Stories of Everyday Things

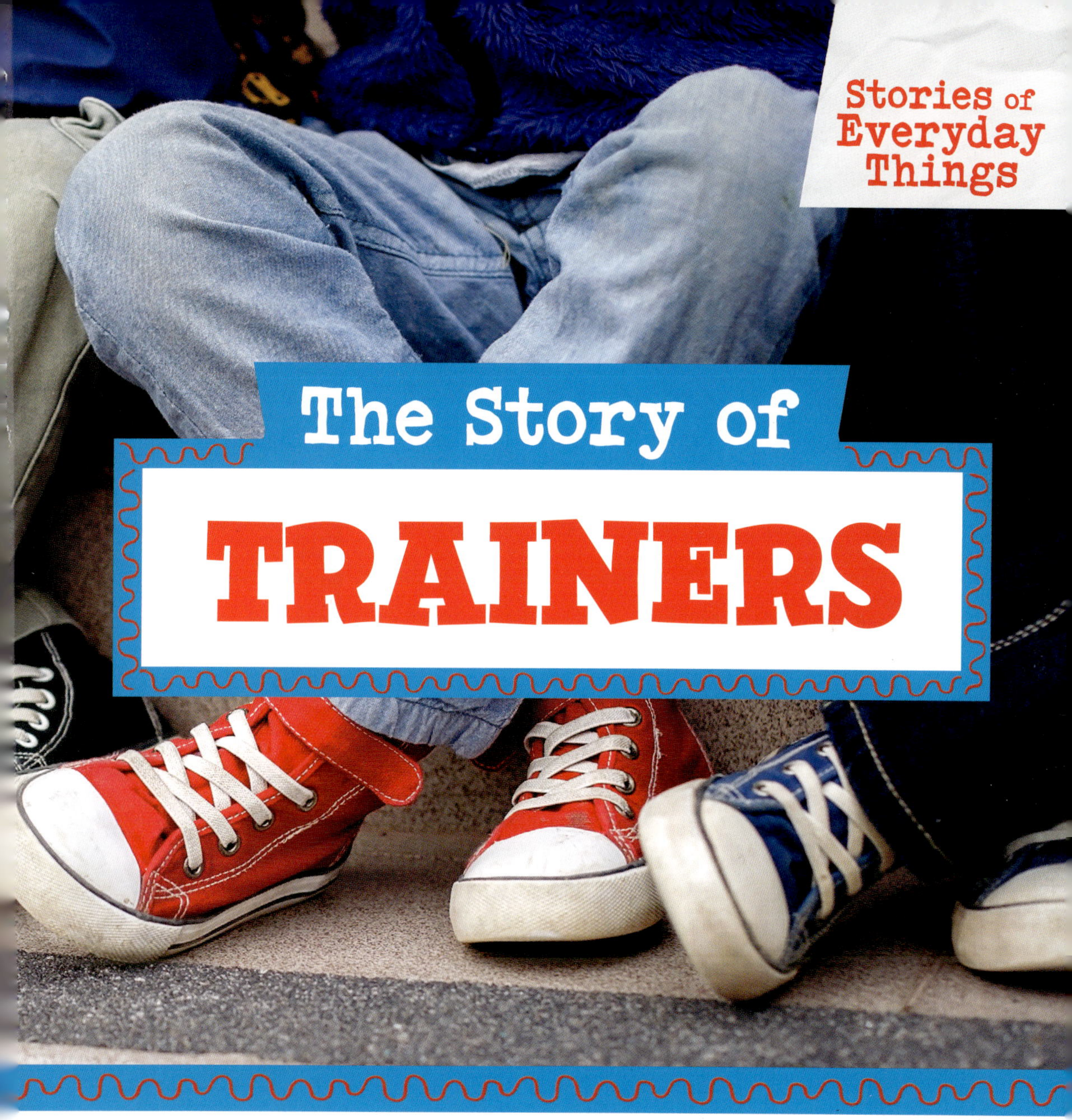

The Story of TRAINERS

by Mae Respicio

raintree
a Capstone company — publishers for children

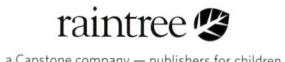

Raintree is an imprint of Capstone Global Library Limited, a company incorporated in England and Wales having its registered office at 264 Banbury Road, Oxford, OX2 7DY – Registered company number: 6695582

www.raintree.co.uk
myorders@raintree.co.uk

Text © Capstone Global Library Limited 2025
The moral rights of the proprietor have been asserted.

All rights reserved. No part of this publication may be reproduced in any form or by any means (including photocopying or storing it in any medium by electronic means and whether or not transiently or incidentally to some other use of this publication) without the written permission of the copyright owner, except in accordance with the provisions of the Copyright, Designs and Patents Act 1988 or under the terms of a licence issued by the Copyright Licensing Agency, 5th Floor, Shackleton House, 4 Battle Bridge Lane, London, SE1 2HX (www.cla.co.uk). Applications for the copyright owner's written permission should be addressed to the publisher.

Editorial credits
Edited by: Alison Deering
Designed by: Jaime Willems
Media Research by: Jo Miller
Production by: Whitney Schaefer
Originated by Capstone Global Library Ltd

ISBN 978 1 3982 5891 4

British Library Cataloguing in Publication Data
A full catalogue record for this book is available from the British Library.

Acknowledgements
We would like to thank the following for permission to reproduce photographs: Alamy: Pictures Now, 10; Getty Images: Hulton Archive, 7, kvkirillov, 8; Shutterstock: 2p2play, 11, 8th.creator, 26, cunaplus, 19, dreamnikon, 20, EmilioZehn, 15, i viewfinder, 21, Itxu, 9, Back Cover, Lithiumphoto, 14, LittleMiss, Cover, Master1305, 5, Myroslava Gerber, 24, panpote, 18, pio3, 22, Roman Samborskyi, 13, ShutterBri, 27, Simikov, 16, Studio Romantic, 17, Tada Images, 25, Tomsickova Tatyana, 1, 23, Yuriy Golub, 29; SuperStock: Science Museum/SSPL/Science and Society, 6
Design Elements: Shutterstock: Luria, Pooretat moonsana

All product and company names are trademarks™ or registered® trademarks of their respective holders.

Every effort has been made to contact copyright holders of material reproduced in this book. Any omissions will be rectified in subsequent printings if notice is given to the publisher.

All the internet addresses (URLs) given in this book were valid at the time of going to press. However, due to the dynamic nature of the internet, some addresses may have changed, or sites may have changed or ceased to exist since publication. While the author and publisher regret any inconvenience this may cause readers, no responsibility for any such changes can be accepted by either the author or the publisher.

Printed and bound in India.

Contents

The world of trainers 4

Trainers through time 6

Creating cool trainers 14

Getting trainers to you 20

Trainers in the spotlight 24

    Decorate your own trainers! 28

    Glossary 30

    Find out more 31

    Index 32

    About the author 32

Words in **bold** appear in the glossary.

The world of trainers

Put your trainers on. Lace them up. Run around. Show off your style!

People all around the world wear trainers. They are worn on playgrounds and on sports pitches. They are even seen on the red carpet! Trainers are a part of everyday life. But how did they become so popular?

Trainers through time

Trainers have been around since the 1800s. In 1832, American Wait Webster **patented** plimsolls. These shoes were made of cloth. Their soles were made of rubber. They had no right or left foot!

An early version of plimsolls cut in half to show the rubber sole.

Things started changing in 1839. An inventor called Charles Goodyear discovered a new process. It was called **vulcanization**. It turned rubber into a flexible material. This made shoes more comfortable. It was also one step towards inventing the trainer.

Charles Goodyear

A pair of Keds

In 1916, the United States Rubber Company created another kind of trainer. They were called Keds. At first, they were called Peds. This came from the Latin word for feet. But another company already had that name. Eventually the name Keds stuck!

Keds were designed for sport. The tops were made from thick **canvas**. The soles were made from sturdy rubber. Rubber soles gave the shoes a much better grip. In 1917, Keds became the first trainers to be **mass-produced**.

The Converse Rubber Shoe Company factory

The real game changer in trainer making was a man called Marquis Converse. He worked at the US Rubber Company. But in 1908, he started the Converse Rubber Shoe Company. In 1917, he created the Converse All Star.

Basketball player and salesman Charles "Chuck" Taylor later promoted the shoe. He helped to make Converse All Stars famous. These trainers are some of the most **iconic** in sporting history. They are still made today.

Many popular brands also make sport trainers. Two of the most famous are Nike and Adidas.

Nike and Adidas are some of today's most popular trainer brands.

In the early 1900s, people wore trainers mostly for sport. But that changed in the 1950s. People began wearing them for a different reason – fashion.

Hollywood actor James Dean was known to wear Converse All Stars. This made trainers even more popular, especially with young people.

In the United States, trainers are called sneakers. Where does the word sneaker come from? It comes from how quiet the shoes are. That's because of the rubber. Sneakers let you sneak up on people!

Creating cool trainers

Today, trainers are not just for sport. They look cool too! Every trainer starts with a design. Designers think about style and shape. They also consider comfort. They make models and **mock-ups**.

A designer cuts out a pattern for a pair of shoes.

Next, it's on to the factory! Each trainer needs a **mould**. This is called a shoe last. What shape is it in? A foot! This helps every trainer to fit properly.

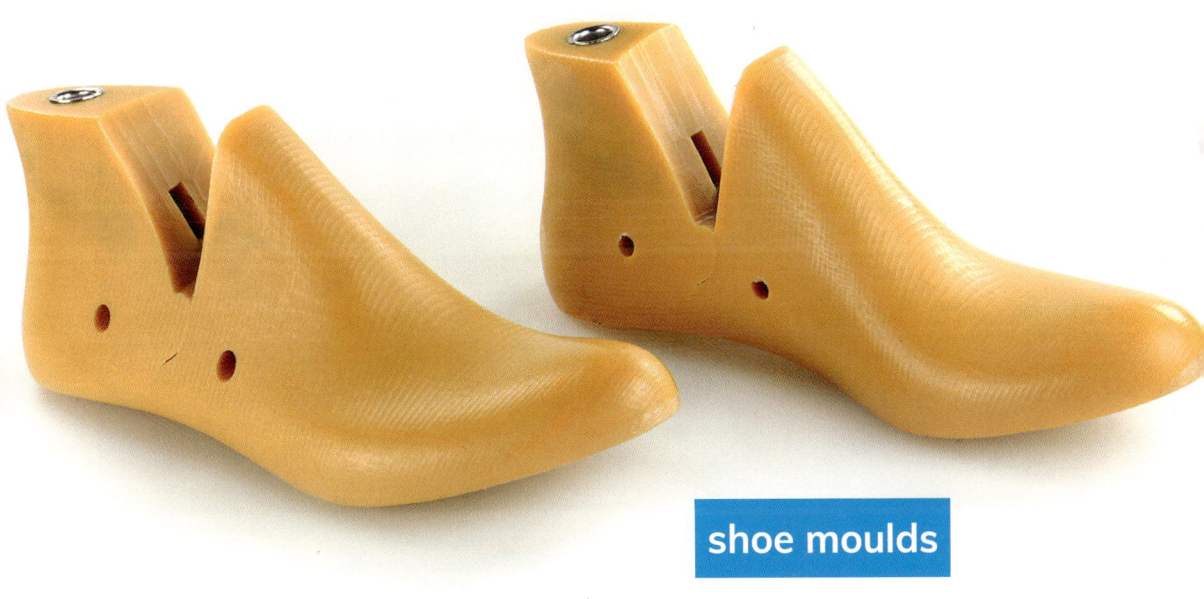

shoe moulds

Trainers are made from raw materials. These can include leather and **synthetic** fabrics. Rubber is used for the soles.

shoe soles

A factory worker uses machinery to create a new pair of shoes.

It takes people and machines to make trainers. Laser machines cut the materials. This makes different parts. There is the top part. The bouncy bottom is the outsole. The middle is the midsole. It is a type of cushion. What for? Comfort.

Next, the parts are stitched together. This is often done by hand. The parts move through an **assembly line**. People use machines to put all the pieces together.

Laces come next. They are added to each shoe. Every trainer is inspected. Is the stitching correct? Is the **logo** in the proper place? Check!

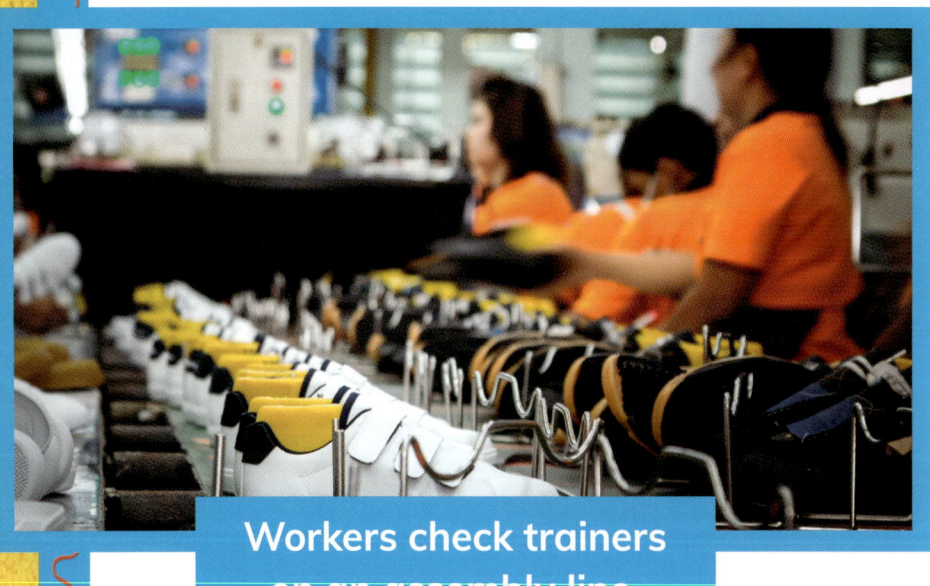
Workers check trainers on an assembly line.

Last step? Packaging. People put the trainers into cardboard boxes. The labels on each box show the size and logo.

Getting trainers to you

How do trainers get from the factory to you? **Distribution**. Boxes of trainers are loaded onto lorries. Some are shipped in containers. Some go directly to shops. Most will go to warehouses and distribution centres.

What are distribution centres? It is where trainers from different factories come together. Why? To sort them. This is done by **conveyor belt**.

Boxes move down a conveyor belt.

Next comes another journey. This time to the shops. Once again, the boxes are loaded onto lorries, ships and planes.

Some trainers are shipped locally. Others travel far. They go to shops all over the world.

Now are they ready to be worn? Soon! First you must choose your trainers. You can shop online. Or you can visit a shop. At last, your trainers have reached you!

Trainers in the spotlight

Today, trainers are very popular. In 2023, UK households spent about £11.8 billion on footwear. Most people own at least one pair of trainers.

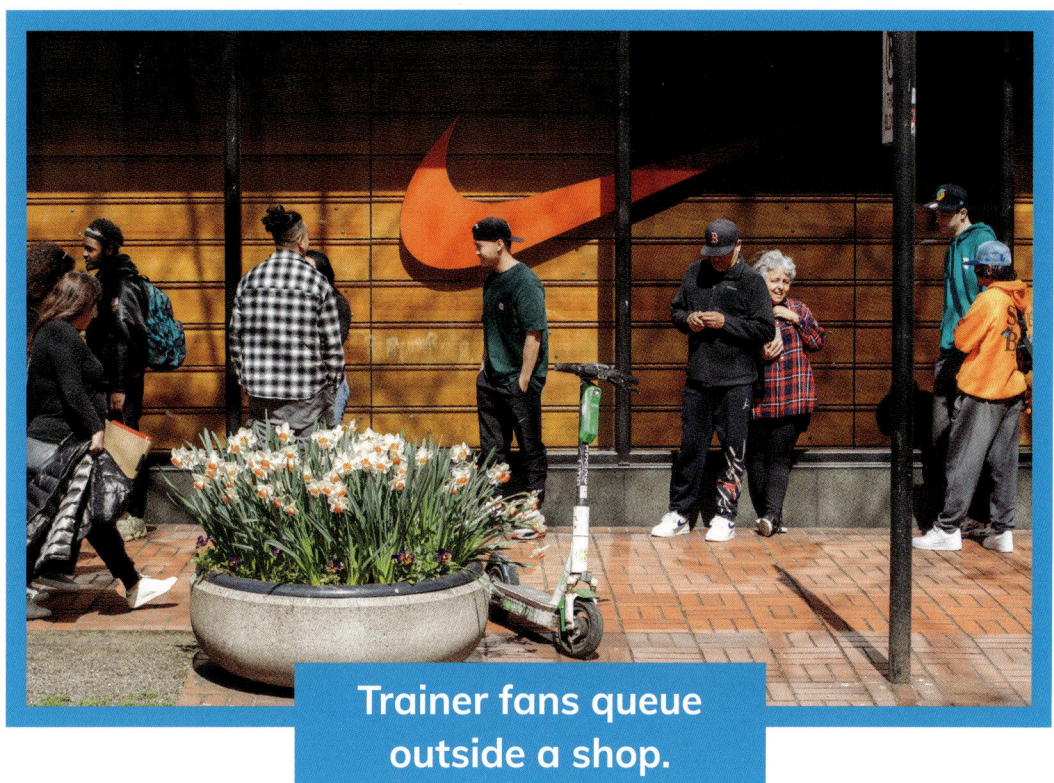

Trainer fans queue outside a shop.

What brand sells the most trainers around the world? Nike. They sell more than 780 million pairs each year. Some fans collect their trainers.

A display of Nike Jordan shoes

Some athletes have trainers named after them. One famous trainer is the Air Jordan. These are named after basketball player Michael Jordan. The logo shows him going for a slam dunk!

Whatever you wear them for, one thing is clear. People around the world wear and love trainers. They are a part of our everyday lives.

Decorate your own trainers!

Anyone can design their own trainers! All it takes is creativity, colour and a blank pair of trainers.

What you need

- paper
- fabric marker pens
- paintbrush
- acrylic paints
- a pair of white canvas trainers

What you do

1. Brainstorm your design on paper. Express your own style!

2. Use fabric marker pens and acrylic paints to draw your design on your trainers. Follow the directions on the fabric marker pens to create your design.

3. To help your design dry, you might need to use a hair dryer. Ask an adult for help.

4. Slip on your trainers. Show them off!

Glossary

assembly line arrangement of workers in a factory; work passes from one person to the next person until the job is done

canvas strong, heavy cloth

conveyor belt mechanical device for carrying items from place to place

distribution act or process of giving out or delivering something

iconic widely recognized and respected

logo symbol of a company's brand

mass-produce make products in large quantities by using machines and dividing work to be done into simpler tasks

mock-up full-size example of a planned design

mould model of an object

patent process of obtaining a legal document to have the right to make or sell a product

synthetic something that is from materials made by people rather than materials found in nature

vulcanization industrial process that strengthens natural rubber

Find out more

BOOKS

Kay's Incredible Inventions, Adam Kay (Puffin, 2024)

You Are History, Greg Jenner (Walker Books, 2024)

You Can Work in Fashion (You Can Work in the Arts), Samantha S. Bell (Raintree, 2019)

WEBSITES

kids.britannica.com/students/article/shoe/277037
Read more about the history of shoes.

www.bbc.co.uk/newsround/av/51069047
Watch this BBC Newsround video to see how trainers are made.

www.beano.com/quiz/personality/best-trainers-2019
What type of trainer are you?! Find out with this fun quiz on the Beano website.

Index

Adidas 11
assembly lines 18
Converse 10–11, 12
Dean, James 12
design 14
distribution 20, 21, 22
factories 15, 17, 21
fashion 12
Goodyear, Charles 7
Jordan, Michael 26
Keds 8–9
logos 18, 19, 26
materials 16
moulds 15
Nike 11, 25, 26
parts 17, 18
plimsolls 6
rubber 6, 7, 9, 13, 16
sport 4, 9, 12, 14
Taylor, Charles 11
United States Rubber Company 8, 10
vulcanization 7
Webster, Wait 6

About the author

Mae Respicio is a non-fiction writer and author whose novel, *The House That Lou Built*, won an Asian/Pacific American Libraries Association Honor award. Mae lives with her family in California, USA, and some of her favourite everyday things include books, beaches and ube ice cream.